Consuming Fire...

Light of Love

Thirty-One Days of God's Glorious Light

Carol Delvic Burchett

CROSSBOOKS
PUBLISHING

CrossBooks™
A Division of LifeWay
1663 Liberty Drive
Bloomington, IN 47403
www.crossbooks.com
Phone: 1-866-879-0502

First published by CrossBooks 12/30/2013

ISBN: 978-1-4627-3424-5 (sc)
ISBN: 978-1-4627-3423-8 (hc)
ISBN: 978-1-4627-3425-2 (e)

Library of Congress Control Number: 2013923777

Printed in the United States of America.

This book is printed on acid-free paper.

"Who alone has immortality,

dwelling in unapproachable light,

whom no man has seen

or can see,

to whom be honor

and everlasting power.

Amen"

1 Timothy 6:16

This book is dedicated to
Patrick A. Burchett,
My wonderful husband and blessing from God,
Our two daughters
Melissa and Melanie,
And our two grandsons
Nick and Christian

Other Books by Carol Delvic Burchett

From Shadows to Shekinah
God's Garden of Love

Preface

"Consuming Fire...Light of Love" is a thirty one day devotional work reflecting the many aspects of God's glorious light. Like an eternal prism, His magnificent light is multifaceted, constantly revealing to us the immeasurable attributes of His character. And the amazing part is that His light is totally and completely accessible to all who seek it in Jesus Christ through the power of the Holy Spirit.

Jesus said in Matthew 7:7-8,
"Ask, and it will be given to you;
seek, and you will find;
knock, and it will be opened to you.
For everyone who asks receives,
and he who seeks finds,
and to him who knocks it will be opened."

This is a promise to you directly from the God who spoke the universe into existence. He is big enough to be everywhere at once yet cares so very deeply for you, individually. His Light is a brilliant key, allowing you to unlock the door of your heart and thereby enter quietly into His presence. Each day's reading is a combination of exhortation, scripture, poetry and prayer. The book is designed to be used as a daily devotional to help you, the reader maintain a sweet fellowship with the Most High God and be transported to His very throne room by faith.

"Let us therefore come boldly to the throne of grace,
That we may obtain mercy
and find grace to help in time of need."
Hebrews 4:16

Jesus said in Matthew 11:28 -- 30,
"Come to Me, all you who labor and are heavy laden
and I will give you rest.
Take my yoke upon you and learn from Me,
for I am gentle and lowly in heart,
and you will find rest for your souls.
For My yoke is easy and My burden is light."

If you are seeking a closer relationship with God and desire to be filled up with the reality of His presence, follow the words of Jesus written in John 6:35, *"I am the bread of life. He who comes to Me shall never hunger, and he who believes in Me shall never thirst."*

It is His will for all us to freely approach Him and dwell with Him in that place of safety, being captivated by the glory of His being. In John chapter 15, Jesus tells us that we are to abide in Him...

"If you abide in Me and My words abide in you,
you will ask what you desire
and it shall be done for you...
These things I have spoken to you,
that My joy may remain in you,
and that your joy may be full."
John 15:9, 11

Nothing is more valued than to know the absolute joy that arises in our hearts when we come into the presence of God. It is unspeakable joy, which cannot compare to anything here on earth. Since we are by nature creatures of worship, true joy can only be found through actively worshipping God in Spirit and in truth. So many times we give our worship and adoration to man. We idolize sports figures, Hollywood celebrities, and all the while, cast aside the One and only true God with barely a thought. God's word is the faithful guide that leads us to the amazing camaraderie that can occur between you and Him. In that beautiful friendship we find love, joy, peace and all the fruits of the Spirit listed in Galatians 5:22. It is nourishment for our souls. The more we read His Word, the more we hunger for it. And the more we meditate in it, the more we realize how much we desperately yearn for it.

> *"Your word is a lamp to my feet*
> *And a light to my path."*
> *Psalm 119:105*

> *"Your words were found and I ate them,*
> *And You word was to me*
> *the joy and rejoicing of my heart."*
> *Jeremiah 15:16*

> *"But you are a chosen generation,*
> *a royal priesthood, a holy nation,*
> *His own special people,*
> *that you may proclaim the praises of Him*
> *who called you out of darkness*
> *into His marvelous light;*
> *who once were not a people*
> *but now are the people of God,*
> *who had not obtained mercy*
> *but now have obtained mercy."*
> *1 Peter 2:9-10*

His extraordinary love for you is not bound by the dimensions of time and space. It is all-encompassing and breath-taking. Step into the light of God's presence today and know the peace that surpasses all understanding. Listen intently for His voice, seek His face and

He will draw near to you. He is the bright and morning star and the complete lover of your soul.

> *"Yes, I have loved you with*
> *An everlasting love;*
> *Therefore with loving kindness*
> *I have drawn you."*
> *Jeremiah 31:3*

Contents

Day One

O Beautiful Face

Long ago, on a day when darkness seemed to have enveloped my life, I felt as if I could not go on another moment. It was then that I sought the face of God. Although I was alone in a place of darkest despair, His presence continued to woo me toward the sphere of His marvelous light. Staring intently at a star filled sky, I called loudly and boldly upon the name of the Lord. As I looked upward into the twinkling night for any possible answer, I became overwhelmed by the view of eternity and infinity which stood before me.

__"Be still and know that I am God,"__ a reply came from inside my head. Yes, the words of Psalm 48:10, echoed quietly there in the dark, whispering words of hope and love. It was then I discovered that it is when you are at the darkest point in life that the light of God seems to shine its brightest. And at that very moment in time, the glory of the Most High God surrounded me and filled me with His Wonderful Light, illuminating my pathway back to Him.

The cold, dampness around me was suddenly replaced by the gloriously beautiful face of Jesus. It was as if He held me close to Him as I leaned into the brightness of His Spirit, taking in the almost tangible presence of His love. Nothing can transcend the joy I felt as I stood there basking in the rays of His hope.

"He is the image of the invisible God,
the firstborn over all creation.
For by Him all things were created
that are in heaven
And on earth, visible and invisible...
__all things were created__
__through Him and for Him.__

And He is before all things,
and in Him all things consist."

Colossians 1:15-17

Seek Him now and you too will find Him. That is a guarantee directly from the word of God.

"... you will seek the Lord your God,
and you will find Him
if you seek Him with all your heart
and with all your soul."

Deuteronomy 4:29

"For it is God who commanded
light to shine
out of darkness
in our hearts to give
the light of the knowledge
of the glory of God
in the face of Jesus Christ."

1 Corinthians. 4:6

"O Beautiful Face"

O beautiful face, O glorious face,
Your wondrous light sublime,
All darkness erased, by your awesome grace,
Throughout the portals of time.

God commanded the light in the darkness to shine,
Reflecting its glow in our hearts,
It's beautiful rays, for now and always,
Like the rivers of warmth it imparts.

His perfect love is magnified, His Deity personified,
All payment for sin is satisfied
By the shedding of his precious blood,

His glory forever will abide, Within our spirits, now purified,
Because of Him, we're justified,
Washed by the cleansing flood.

O beautiful face, our lives You embrace,
The glory of God is revealed,
Throughout time and space, in this marvelous place,
Our salvation eternally sealed.

Forever to walk in the rays of Your glory,
Being cradled in Your outstretched hands,
Unconditional love is your incredible story,
So perfect are all Your plans.

Precious Heavenly Father,

We seek your glorious face today
and ask that You reveal
the glory of Your Presence to us once again.
Our request is that Your face would
shine upon us disclosing to us
Your perfect Light.
In Jesus name...
Amen.

"Fire and Cloud"

"In the daytime also He led them with a cloud,
And all the night with a light of fire."
Psalm 78:14

O, Lord please show me your perfect way,
That I may hear Your voice,
Help me distinguish the night from day,
Let my hungry heart rejoice.

At night, You display Your awesome fire,
And by day, Your protecting cloud,
They are ever before me, yet I still inquire,
And call to You aloud.

Your way is directed by cloud and flame,
So clear to the naked eye,
Yet my murmur to You is still the same,
As if I cannot see the sky.

I'll trust in You with all my heart,
And lean not on my own understanding,
My faithless cry will thus depart,
As my reliance on You is expanding.

In all my ways, I'll acknowledge You,
So Your paths to me, You'll show,
Only then can I see your light so true,
You guide me as I go.

"Trust in the Lord with all your heart,
and lean not on your own understanding.
In all your ways acknowledge Him
and He will direct your paths."
Proverbs 3:5-6

Dear Lord,

We thank you for providing the perfect sacrifice for our sin, Your Son Jesus Christ who takes away the sin of the world. You created us with a free will to either accept You or reject You and we pray that all who read this would come to know You even as we are known by You. Thank you for loving us.
In Jesus name...
Amen

Day Three

The Sight of the Glory of God

The Law of Moses could never atone for sin, only the blood of Jesus could pay that great price. He is the only perfect sacrifice for sin and without Him there could be no redemption between a perfect God and sinful imperfect man. He is a glorious God, full of mercy.

Moses said to God in Exodus 33:18:

"Please show me your glory,"
the Lord replied,
"You cannot see My face;
for no man shall see Me and live...
and the Lord said, here is a place by Me,
and you shall stand on the rock.
So shall it be, while my glory passes by,
that I will put you in the cleft of the <u>rock</u>,
and will cover you with My hand while I pass by."

That "rock" is Jesus Christ. He is the only way for us to enter into God's glory, for He tells us this in *John 14:6,*

"I am the way, the truth and the life.
No one comes to the Father, except by Me."

In 1 Corinthians 10:4,
the Apostle Paul also references this Rock when he wrote,

"Moreover, brethren,
I do not want you to be unaware
that all our fathers were under the cloud,
all passed through the sea,
all were baptized into Moses in the cloud and in the sea,
all ate the same spiritual food,

and all drank the same spiritual drink.
For they drank of that spiritual Rock that followed them,
and that Rock was Christ."

"...Who being the brightness of His glory
and the express image of His person,
and upholding all things
by the word of His power,
when He had by Himself purged out sins,
sat down on the right hand of the Majesty on high..."
Hebrews 1:3

"The sight of the glory of the Lord was like
a consuming fire on the top of the mountain..."
Exodus 24:17

The Sight of the Glory of God

Lord, take me to the top of Your mighty mountain,
That I may hear Your voice,
And drink the water of Your living fountain,
Let my seeking heart rejoice.

Speak to me Your wondrous word,
Open my ears to the sound,
The most loving sound ear has ever heard,
Let my love for You abound.

My desire is to hear Your voice on high,
Drawing closer to my core,
To hear your whispered lullaby,
As it flows from heaven's shore.

You are, oh so high and lifted up,
My strength and lofty tower,
Your living water fills my cup,
Your word calls forth Your power.

A consuming fire with tongues of flame,
Your glory will forever shine,
I magnify Your Holy Name,
And give thanks that You are mine.

To gaze on your splendor is to live anew,
It's our perfect expectation,
Your spoken Word, forever true,
Unveils Your revelation.

Until Your glory can be revealed,
I'll hide in the cleft of Your Rock,
Loved, protected, sheltered, sealed,
Waiting to hear your knock.

"Behold, I stand at the door and knock.
If anyone hears My voice
and opens the door I will come in to him."
Revelation 3:20

Dear Lord,

How great you are, O God...so mighty, so
magnificent... words cannot describe You.
Your glory penetrates the darkness of earth
Allowing us to see Your Light.
Refine us with Your
holy fire. Remove all the
dross and transform us.
Thank you for visiting us here and
making Your presence known to us.

Day Four

Shining Light

"Let your light so shine before men,
that they may see your good works
and glorify your father in heaven."
Matthew 5:16

Once we become children of God through faith in the blood of Jesus, we are commanded to let His light within us shine, reflecting the true glory of God. More than a few times I have noticed my own lamp beginning to dim and have felt the shadows creeping in once again, trying to rob me of my joy. At those times, when the phantoms of depression weigh heavily on my soul, dragging me into its cave of despair, I remember the voice of David, crying out to the Lord…

"Hear my cry, O God: Attend to my prayer.
From the end of the earth I will cry to You."
Psalm 61:1

"Arise, cry out in the night,
pour out your heart like water
before the face of the Lord."
Lamentations 2:19

In response, our God is <u>always</u> faithful to draw near to us when we sincerely call out to Him from the depths of our hearts.

"But You, O Lord are a shield for me,
My glory and the One who lifts up my head."
Psalm 3:3

"I sought the Lord and He heard me,
and delivered me from all my fears."
Psalm 34:4

"Because You have been my help,
therefore in the shadow of Your wings I will rejoice."
Psalm 63:7

"For You will light my lamp;
The Lord my God
will enlighten my darkness." Psalm 18:28

"Shining Light"

*"But the path of the just is like the shining sun,
that shines brighter unto the perfect day..."*
Proverbs 4:18

From out of the pit of the darkest night,
When hope had drifted on a sea of despair,
A shining Light, a Holy Light,
Made its presence there.

Standing in the midst of a sacred place,
Within the most glorious light of all,
Illumined by Jesus' beautiful face,
I heard the trumpet call.

Glowing beams, warm healing rays,
His light reflecting in my heart,
The Father's glory encamped in praise,
Surround His radiant work of art.

The sun, the stars and flames of fire,
In this world can never compare,
With the Light of Love in bright attire,
As we meet Him in the air.

*"... in which you shine like stars in the universe,
holding out the word of life."*
Philippians 2:15

Dear Lord,

As we sit in Your presence
meditating upon Your shining
light, we pray we would draw closer to you
and feel the greatness of your love.
Your light is our guide that shows
us the path to your love.
We thank You and praise you from the
bottom of our hearts for who You are.

Amen

Day Five

The Brightness of His Glory

Throughout the centuries many have wondered about the person of Jesus Christ; who He really is and why He came. Was He God? Was He merely a good man? Was He just a Jewish prophet? Was it all only a fable? Everyone seems to have a strong opinion concerning Him, even those who do not believe in Him. What other name can cause so much controversy? Why, even in our own country, is the name of Jesus forbidden to be spoken in certain circles? There are so many questions about this Person who defines time by his birth and death.

But the Bible is perfectly clear regarding all of these questions. The first few verses of the gospel of John describe Jesus most accurately when it states:

> *"In the beginning was the Word,*
> *and the Word was with God,*
> *and the Word was God.*
> *He was in the beginning with God.*
> *All things were made by Him,*
> *and without Him nothing was made that was made.*
> *In Him was life and the life was the light of men...*
> *And the Word became flesh and dwelt among us,*
> *And we beheld His glory*
> *as of the only begotten of the Father,*
> *full of grace and truth."*

> *"... who has saved us and called us with a holy calling,*
> *not according to our works,*
> *but according to His own purpose*
> *and grace which was given to us in Christ Jesus*
> *before time began."*
> *2 Timothy 1: 9-10*

"Who being the brightness of His glory
and the express image of His person
and upholding all things by the word of His power..."
Hebrews 1:1-3

The Brightness of His Glory

"Who is Jesus?" you may wonder,
The power of God, His rolling thunder,
The brightness of His Father's glory,
Tell us more of this wondrous story.

The very image of His being,
It's Almighty God that we are seeing,
All is upheld by the word of His power,
The name of the Lord is our strong tower.

Because He alone has purged our sins,
Eternal life with Him begins.
But more that... The Savior sat,
On the Father's right hand, His Majesty so grand...

That all on high could clearly see,
The evidence of His Deity,
And all could hear the Rhapsody,
Amid eternal ecstasy.

With our Blessed Savior we will soar,
In the presence of the One we most adore,
Casting our crowns on heaven's floor,
And so be with Him evermore.

"Blessing and honor and glory and power"
Be to our God this very hour,
And to the One upon the throne,
Be wondrous worship to Him alone,

And to the Lamb forever and ever,
We will sing our praises altogether,
To lift up high His Holy Name,
His awesome glory we proclaim.

"Blessing and honor and glory and power
be to Him who sits on the throne,
And to the lamb forever and ever!"
Revelation 5:13

Dear Lord,

The portal of heaven is open
to us and Your love
covers us from above. How You love
Your children! Not because we are worthy
but because You are love.
Amen

"He who does not love
Does not know God,
For God is Love."

1 John 4:8

Day Six

The Throne

Imagine standing before the Lord as He sits on His glorious throne within the magnificent gates of heaven. Captivating beauty surrounds us while, with our ears we embrace the praises of angels singing a melodious rhapsody. As we gaze upon God's Shekinah glory, we witness a glowing musical sphere, brighter than a thousand suns in a thousand universes. By comparison, the things of earth are merely insignificant shadows, not worthy of acceptance.

"For now we see in a mirror, dimly,
but then face to face.
Now I know in part,
but then I shall know just as I also am known."
1 Corinthians 13:12

"Then I turned to see the voice that spoke to me.
And having turned I saw seven golden lampstands,
and in the midst of the seven lampstands
One like the Son of Man,
clothed with a garment down to His feet
and girded about the chest with a golden band.
His head and hair was white like wool,
as white as snow, and His eyes were like a flame of fire;
His feet were like brass,
as if refined in a furnace,
and His voice as the sound of many waters.
He had in his right hand seven stars,
out of His mouth went a sharp two-edged sword
and His countenance was like the sun shining in its strength.
And when I saw Him, I fell at His feet as dead.
But He laid His right hand on me, saying to me,
"Do not be afraid; I am the First and the Last..."
Revelation 1:10-11

*"Blessing and honor and glory and power Be to Him
who sits on the throne, And to the Lamb, forever and ever!"*
Revelation 5:13

*"I saw the Lord sitting on the throne, high and lifted up,
and the train of his robe filled the temple....
And one cried to another and said:
'Holy, holy, holy is the Lord of hosts;
The whole earth is full of His glory!'"*
Isaiah 6:1-3

Yes, He is waiting for us to call upon Him, to take us to that place
of pure love, to the very throne room of God, where *Hebrews 4:16*
tells us,

*"Let us therefore come boldly
to the throne of grace,
that we may obtain mercy
and find grace to help in time of need."*

*"Your throne, O God is forever and ever;
A scepter of righteousness
Is the scepter of Your kingdom."*
Psalm 45:6

*"The Lord has established
His throne in heaven,
And His kingdom rules over all."*
Psalm 103:19

*"Immediately, I was in the Spirit,
And behold, a throne set in Heaven,
And One sat on the throne."*
Revelation 4:2

"The Throne"

"Revelation Chapter Four"

"After these things I looked, and behold, a door standing open in heaven. And the first voice which I heard was like a trumpet speaking with me, saying, 'Come up here, and I will show you things which must take place after this.' Immediately I was in the Spirit; and behold, a throne set in heaven and One sat on the throne. And He who sat there was like a jasper and a sardius stone in appearance; and there was a rainbow around the throne, in appearance like an emerald. Around the throne were twenty-four thrones, and on the thrones I saw twenty-four elders sitting, clothed in white robes; and they had crowns of gold on their heads. And from the throne proceeded lightenings, thunderings and voices. Seven lamps of fire were burning before the throne, which are the seven Spirits of God. Before the throne was a sea of glass, like crystal. And in the midst of the throne were four living creatures full of eyes in front and in back. The first living creature was like a lion, the second living creature like a calf, the third living creature had a face like a man, and the fourth living creature was like a flying eagle. The four living creatures, each having six wings, were full of eyes around and within. And they do not rest day or night, saying:

'Holy, holy, holy,
Lord God Almighty,
Who was and is and is to come!'

Whenever the living creatures give glory and honor and thanks to Him who sits on the throne, who lives forever and ever, the twenty-four elders fall down before Him who sits on the throne and worship Him who lives forever and ever, and cast their crowns before the throne, saying:

'You are worthy, O Lord,
To receive glory and honor and power;
For You created all things,
And by Your will they exist
And were created.'

"The Throne"

I looked and saw the door ajar,
And heard a voice like a trumpet blowing,
He called me to the heavens afar,
In the Spirit, I saw Him glowing.

"Come up here," the voice was speaking,
"I'll show what is to come,"
Ascending to the throne and seeking,
My inward soul was overcome.

In my spirit I saw a wondrous throne,
In the midst of heaven's floor,
And He who sat there was my own,
The One I most adore.

In the appearance of many precious stones,
Magnificent to the eye,
Surrounded by twenty four more thrones,
The angels sang a lullaby.

Before the throne was a sea like glass,
With four creatures in its midst,
Their wings were fluttering extremely fast,
Without rest, they forever exist.

"Holy, Holy, Holy", they sang,
From the throne, the thunder crashed,
Throughout the sphere, their voices rang,
Great and powerful lightening flashed.

As the creatures gave glory and honor and praise,
Elders casting their crowns at the feet,
Of the One on the throne, full of power and grace,
Their worship for Him is complete.

Endless choruses ring throughout the portals of time,
"You are worthy, O Lord", they sounded,
"To receive glory and honor and power, sublime,"
By this scene, I was so astounded.

Dear Lord,

We thank You, that we have complete
access to Your throne room through
Your Son, Jesus Christ. You visit us here
and fill us with Your presence. Radiant beams
stream down from Your dwelling place.
You are full of glory.

Amen

Day Seven

Glory to God in the highest

"For unto us a child is born, unto us a son is given;
And the government will be upon His shoulder.
And His name will be called Wonderful,
Counselor, Mighty God, Everlasting Father,
Prince of Peace."
Isaiah 9:6

These words written by Isaiah the prophet, were actually scripted hundreds of years before the birth of Jesus; yet paint such an accurate and precise portrait of Him. So it is with many other Old Testament prophets who predicted everything from where He would be born (Micah 5:2), what He would look like (Isaiah 53:2) to the brutality of His death (Isaiah 53:4-8)

The sole purpose of His life on earth was that through His death He could atone for our sins, reconciling sinful man to a perfect God. He was Almighty God who took on the form of human flesh that He might become the complete sacrifice for us.

"For He (God), made Him (Christ) who knew no sin
to be sin for us, that we might become
the righteousness of God in Him."
2 Corinthians 5:21

"… giving thanks to the Father who has qualified us
to be partakers of the inheritance of the saints in the light.
He has delivered us from the power of darkness
and conveyed us into the kingdom of the Son of His love,
in whom we have redemption, through his blood,
the forgiveness of sins.
Colossians 1:12:14

"And the Word became flesh and dwelt among us, and we beheld His glory, the glory as of the only begotten of the Father, full of grace and truth."
John 1:14

"Glory to God in the Highest"

"And suddenly there was with the angel,
a multitude of the heavenly host,
praising God and saying
Glory to God in the highest..."
Luke 2:13 & 14

On the sacred night of our Savior's birth,
That night in a manger so damp and cold,
Deity in glory, descended to earth,
Many ancient prophecies in Him, foretold.

So long ago in a star filled sky,
While shepherds tended their flocks,
A radiant beam appeared on High,
Its majesty illuminating the sand and rocks.

In awe they followed the brightest star,
Faithfully through the night,
With many, they traveled from near and far,
Pursuing this magnificent Light.

An angel appeared with tidings of joy,
He had the greatest message to bestow,
A king was born, a baby boy,
The One promised so long ago.

Radiance flowed from the Infant's face,
Revealing God's glory to all,
Surrounding them with His boundless grace,
His holiness to men would befall.

The sky was alive with the heavenly host,
"Glory to God in the highest", they cried,
The Father, the Son and the Holy Ghost,
In a splendor that cannot be denied.

A child is born, a son is given,
Wonderful Counselor is His name,
Almighty God has come from heaven,
The Prince of Peace all will proclaim.

God set this time in history,
To reconcile Himself to man,
Revealing His greatest mystery,
Complete redemption was His plan.

"Christ has redeemed us from the law,
Having become a curse for us
(for it is written, Cursed is everyone
Who hangs on a tree'),
That the blessing of Abraham
May come upon the Gentiles in Jesus Christ,
That we might receive the promise
Of the Spirit through faith."

Galatians 3:13-14

Dear Lord,

We are so grateful for your perfect redemption.
You entered the world as a human baby, grew
into a man, felt all of the things we feel and
yet remained without sin. Your word gives us
such sweet comfort. "Tidings of
comfort and joy."
We are wrapped in Your peaceful presence.
and know You are forever with us.
We rest in Your complete love.
Because of Your perfect sacrifice,
we are reconciled to You forever.

Amen

Day Eight

Who is like You?

"Yours, O Lord, is the greatness, the power and the glory,
The victory and the majesty;
For all that is in heaven and earth are Yours."
1 Chronicles 29:11

There is no one like our God. It is He who dwells in unapproachable light and loved us enough to visit us in our time of greatest need. He is the one who hung the universe, stretching it out to infinity, yet all the while showing us the magnitude of His unconditional love. Then He stretched His arms out on the cross for us that we might have eternal life through Him.

"Have you not known?
Have you not heard?
Has it not been told you from the beginning?
Have you not understood
from the foundations of the earth?
Isaiah 40: 21-22

"O Lord, my God, You are very great:
You are clothed with honor and majesty,
Who cover Yourself with light as with a garment"
Psalm 104:1-2

Yes, it is He who carries us on the wings of the fire of God's glory, to the place he has prepared for each one of us individually; to a place that goes beyond time and space and all the elements of earth, to the home where we dwell with Him forever.

"Eye has not seen, nor ear heard,
nor have entered into the heart of man
the things which God has prepared
for those who love Him.
But God has revealed them to us through His Spirit.
For the Spirit searches all things,
yes, the deep things of God."
1 Corinthians 2:9-10

"Who is Like You"

*"Who is like You, majestic in holiness,
awesome in glory, working wonders?
...In your unfailing love You will lead
the people you have redeemed."
Exodus 15:11 & 13*

Who is like you, Precious Lord?
Majestic in holiness, awesome in glory,
Our savior, the One who is most adored,
Creation proclaims your wondrous story.

Your righteous right hand has worked such wonders,
Brilliant light shines from Your core,
Through loving words, Your power thunders,
Displaying Your might forevermore.

Yet unfailing love surrounds Your being,
Leading us to Your throne of grace,
It's only Your adoring face I'm seeing,
I feel content in Your warm embrace.

Who is like You, Majestic Savior?
None else can give a love so true,
Revealing mercy with untold favor,
Not one can care as much as You.

Who is like You, majestic and holy,
Redeeming Your children in perfect love,
Extending Your grace to the weak and lowly,
You are awesome in glory, and pure as a dove.

Dear Lord,

You are the God of all creation, for by You
all things in heaven and earth were made...
both visible and invisible.
You have always been here,
yet you chose to create
us for Your glory. You placed
us in a special space called earth
and formed a special dimension for us
called time. One day we will
leave all this behind and dwell
with You in unapproachable light.

Amen

Day Nine

My Abba

Darkness has been described as the lack or deficiency of light. Not so much an entity in itself, but the antithesis of an entity. The word of God has a lot to say about darkness and the despair that follows it. But it has even more to say about God's glorious light.

"Jesus spoke to them again, saying, I am the light of the world.
He who follows Me shall not walk in
darkness but have the light of life."
John 8:12

Darkness denotes coldness, evil and fear, while light brings to mind brilliance, radiance, warmth and glory. Which would you prefer to dwell in for all eternity? The choice belongs to each of us and the decision we make will determine our fate forever.

"Choose for yourselves this day,
whom you will serve...
but as for me and my house,
we will serve the Lord."
Joshua 14-15

"God is light and in Him is no darkness at all...
walk in the light as He is in the light."
1 John 1:7

God's light is ever with us, dispelling the shadows of this world, conquering all darkness and taking us into the very presence of His majesty.

"then your light shall dawn in the darkness,
And your darkness shall be as the noonday.
The Lord will guide you continually,

And satisfy your soul in drought,
And strengthen your bones;
You shall be like a watered garden,
And like a spring of water,
whose waters do not fail"
Isaiah 58:10-11

"My Abba"

The hand of fear tightly gripped my soul,
My world was dark, empty and bare,
The wounds of time had taken their toll,
My life was filled with bleak despair.

Then my voice was heard in the blackest night,
In faith I called on the Name of the Lord,
He came and rescued me from my plight,
His loving Spirit on me was poured.

No more are my steps encased in fear,
No more to walk this world alone,
For my Abba, my Father abides so near,
My heart is His and not my own.

From out of bondage He has set us free,
No longer slaves but daughters and sons,
Only His loving face I see,
His redeeming work in me is done.

Not of myself for I am undeserving,
But through His blood that was shed for me,
Through His mighty power and love, unswerving,
Now His precious daughter I can be.

"Because you are sons,
God sent the Spirit of His Son into our hearts,
the Spirit who calls out, 'Abba, Father'.
So you are no longer a slave
but a Son..."

Galatians 4: 6 & 7

Dear Lord,

You are truly our Abba Father and we are
Your children. We cherish the special times
in which you manifest yourself to us in such a
personal way. You are Almighty God
yet you still desire fellowship of Your precious
children. We love you with all that is within us.

Amen

Day Ten

Your Holy Name

The word of God has much to say about the absolute power and glory that is revealed in the name of our God. His light shines brightly, exposing the darkness created by the fall of man, and revealing the light of who He is. There is incredible power in the name of God.

"Therefore God also has exalted Him
and given Him the name which is above every name,
that at the name of Jesus every knee should bow,
of those in heaven, and of those on earth,
and of those under the earth,
that every tongue should confess that Jesus is Lord,
to the glory of God the Father."
Philippians 2:9-11

Volumes have been written concerning the many names of God listed in scripture and all of these names describe His holy attributes. Just a few of these are listed below:

Adonai – The Lord
El Elyon - The God Most High
Elohim – The God of creation
El Roi – The God who sees
El Shadaii – The all sufficient One
Emmanuel – God with us
Jehovah – The self existent One
Jesus – The name above all names,
Jehovah-Jireh – The Lord who provides

There are so many more names for God are scattered within the pages of the Bible and each of them is a praise within itself, for the wonderful God that we serve. His name is to be forever praised.

"Praise the Lord! Praise of servants of the Lord,
Praise the name of the Lord
from this time forth and forevermore!
From the rising of the sun to its going down
The Lord's name is to be praised."
Psalm 113: 1-3

"Your Holy Name"

"Who shall not fear You,
O Lord, and glorify Your name?
For You alone are holy."
Revelation 15:4

Your Holiness is brighter than a trillion lights,
Your name be glorified without end,
Your presence illumines the darkest of nights,
Revealing the Radiance Your glow transcends.

Your holy name is above the clouds,
More magnificent than we can know,
Surpassing all that man endows,
Filling our souls with all You bestow.

How excellent is Your name upon earth,
You have set Your glory in the universe,
Presenting to us your astounding worth,
While Your gifts to mankind You continually disperse.

Who shall not fear you and glorify Your name?
For You alone are holy,
In the bounds of love, You're a consuming flame,
We long to ever know Thee.

Your name is called The Word of God,
And the armies in heaven will follow,
From Your mouth, the sharpest Sword will trod,
That the kings of earth will swallow.

"He was clothed with a robe dipped in blood,
and His name is called The Word of God.
And the armies in heaven,
clothed in fine linen, white and clean,
followed Him on white horses.
Now out of His mouth goes a sharp sword..."
Revelation 19:13

Dear Lord,

We are in awe of You! Your name is
above any name in heaven and
earth. Mere man cannot fathom
Your greatness.
We bask in Your glory.

Amen

Day Eleven

Praise

"The Lord is great and greatly to be praised."
1 Chronicles 16:25

To the all-powerful creator of the universe and lover of my soul:

How great and mighty is our God! We stand before You with our hands lifted high because You are worthy of all our praise. Shining light surrounds You and its reflection is ever apparent within our hearts. Worshiping You brings us unspeakable joy as we are embraced in the brilliance of Your Glory. How magnificent You are in all Your splendor. In my mind's eye, no matter how hard I try to see Your true beauty, I can see only a glimpse and shadow of Your greatness. I look forward to the day when I can walk in your presence and be totally engulfed in Your love. I praise You with all that is in me.

Words are so inadequate in attempting to communicate our praise for our Lord. Fortunately for us, He sees our hearts and is able to distinguish the depth of our feelings for Him.

"Sing to the Lord, all the earth;
Proclaim the good news of his salvation
from day to day.
Declare His glory among the nations,
His wonders among all peoples.
For the Lord is great
and greatly to be praised."
1 Chronicles 16:23-25

"I will bless the Lord at all times;
His praise shall continually be in my mouth.
My soul shall make its boast in the LORD;
The humble shall hear of it and be glad.
Oh, magnify the LORD with me,
And let us exalt His name forever."
Psalm 34: 1-3

"Praise"

"Because your love is better than life,
my lips will glorify You."
Psalm 63:3

Your love is better than life itself,
Although life is the best that we know,
The light of your face,
The height of your grace,
And the bountiful joy You bestow,

I stand in awe and give You praise,
As I stare toward heaven and the One You raised,
Your love is unending,
Your Spirit transcending,
It comforts us through our remainder of days.

On earth You protect us,
In heaven You perfect us,
While holding our lives in the palms of Your hands,
Your power restores us,
Your Spirit implores us,
The universe bows at your slightest command.

Our creator, redeemer, our Savior and friend,
To You alone, our praises ascend,
Our exaltation will soar,
To the One we adore,
Forever and ever, Amen

"Oh magnify the Lord with me,
And let us exalt His name together."
Psalm 34:4

Dear Lord,

You are so worthy to be praised!

Amen

"I will praise the Lord
According to His righteousness,
I will sing praise to the name
O the Lord Most High."

Psalm 7:17

Day Twelve

That Blessed Hope

"To them God willed to make known
what are the riches of the glory of this mystery...
which is Christ in you, the hope of glory."
Romans 5:2

We have no hope within ourselves, being once alienated from God (Colossians 1: 19-23), but now through Jesus Christ, we are completely reconciled. Ephesians 2:12 says that we were *"without hope and without God in the world"*.

"For You are my hope, O Lord GOD;
You are my trust from my youth."
Psalm 70:5

We look forward to the day when we meet Him in the air and will be with Him forevermore. This is truly the blessed hope that 1 Corinthians 5:22 speaks about. We will be transformed into His image as we are changed in mid-air.

"Now I say, brethren, that flesh and blood
cannot inherit the kingdom of God;
nor does corruption inherit incorruption.
Behold, I tell you a mystery:
We shall not all sleep, but we shall all be changed
In a moment, in the twinkling of an eye,
at the last trumpet. For the trumpet will sound
And the dead will be raised incorruptible,
and we shall all be changed."
1 Corinthians 15:50-52

"That Blessed Hope"

"Looking for the blessed hope and glorious appearing
of our Great God and Savior Jesus Christ..."
Titus 2:13

That blessed hope of Your glorious appearing,
Gives me strength to raise,
My hands in praise,
My thoughts of You are so endearing,
Your word is all that I am hearing,
Both now and the remainder of my days.

We'll meet in the air in the twinkling of an eye,
That wonderful place,
Where I'll see Your face,
When the clouds will part in the golden sky,
No more questions or wondering why,
Only Your glorious grace.

Will it be tomorrow when we leave this domain?
Only You can know,
As You glance below,
"To live is Christ and to die is gain",
Let only that be my earthly refrain,
As I bask in the love that you bestow.

We must hold on loosely to the things of earth,
With our eyes on You,
You can see us through,
This thin portal to our second birth,
Having nothing to do with our own worth,
As we begin with You our lives anew.

"...in a flash, in the twinkling of an eye,
at the last trumpet, for the dead will be raised imperishable
and we will all be changed..."
I Corinthians 15:52 NIV

Dear Lord,

Thank you for the blessed hope
we have in You.
While we are here on earth,
You continually
Sanctify us and are prepare us for an
eternity in Your majestic presence.
We look forward with great expectation
to what lies ahead.
Words cannot describe our love for You.

Amen

Day Thirteen

I Will Seek You

Seek after the Lord and He will reveal Himself to you. This is a promise to all of us who genuinely seek earnestly for God with our whole heart and sincerely desire the closeness of His companionship. This awesome God, who created the universe, is forever available to us whenever we call upon Him.

"Seek the Lord while he may be found,
Call upon Him while He is near." Isaiah 55:6

So many times we are wrapped up in the trivialities our own world, a world that does not include God. He is far from us because we choose to be far from Him. God tells us in His word that we are to follow <u>hard</u> after Him and to put Him first in our lives, yet our own preoccupation with "self" hinders us from joining in the sweetest fellowship that can ever be encountered this side of heaven. It would be like a child who was raised eating only spinach when all the while ice cream was awaiting him in the next room. So it is with God.

He waits patiently for us to enter into His glorious realm, where we can be totally covered in His love. It is a perfect love which surpasses all understanding. He is always waiting for us to join him, to partake of the river of His living water, to soar with Him on the wings of the wind, to fervently seek His face and listen for the whisper of His voice. All these blessings are just a prayer away, but we must diligently pursue Him and if we do, He promises that He will be found.

"But from there you will seek the Lord your God,
and you will find Him when you seek Him
with all your heart and with all your soul."
Deuteronomy 4:29

Jesus desires for us to enter into His presence and invites us to do so. Take Him up on it and know the complete love, joy and peace that awaits you.

"Come to Me, all you who labor and are heavy laden, and I will give you rest. Take my yoke upon you and learn from Me, for I am meek and lowly in heart, and you will find rest for your souls. For My yoke is easy and My burden is light."
Matthew 11:28-29

"I Will Seek You"

"Oh God, You are my God, Early will I seek You;
My soul thirsts for you, my flesh longs for you
In a dry and thirsty land where there is no water.
So I have looked for You in the sanctuary,
To see Your power and glory."
Psalm 63:1-2

When the sun appears in the morning sky,
My soul pursues Your heart,
Your Holy name I magnify,
As I behold your works of art.

I'll seek Your face, my soul will thirst,
From dawn till setting sun,
Forever, I will put You first,
Until this age is done.

This life is but a desert waste,
Resembling a dry and thirsty land,
Not a drop of water will I taste,
As I trudge through shifting sand.

My flesh and spirit endlessly pine,
For the shadow of Your wings,
For Your glory that will ever shine,
And the brilliance that it brings.

In the sanctuary I search for You
To see Your wonder and power,
Your closeness renews me like the dew,
As water to a wilted flower.

"Glory in His holy name;
let the hearts of those rejoice who seek the Lord!
Seek the Lord and His strength; Seek His face evermore!"
1 Chronicles 16:9-11

O, God,

You are perfect and awesome
beyond all measure.
We long for You to illuminate
our dark and shadowy world.
Yours is the only refreshment we can hope for.
When we abide with You,
Your peace and joy overwhelm us
and Your mighty Spirit
saturates us with living water.
Thank You, Lord.

Amen

Day Fourteen

I Will Call upon the Lord

King David's haunting cry was heard by God when distress and despair had blanketed his life. From the top of the mountains to the floor below, his voice was heard, echoing through the night as he called fiercely upon the name of the Lord. But his thundering cries were also heard in times of extreme joy, when he would call out to his God and Savior in praise, worship and blessing from the bottom of his heart.

"I will love You, O Lord, my strength.
The Lord is my Rock and my fortress and my deliverer;
My God, my strength, in whom I will trust;
My shield and the horn of my salvation, my stronghold.
I will call on the Lord who is worthy to be praised."
Psalm 18:1-3

"I will bless the Lord at all times:
His praise will continually be in my mouth."
Psalm 34:1

When we call upon Him, He is always there for us, truly desiring our fellowship. This is how much our Lord loves us, that in spite of our sins, His arms are always open to us, drawing us to Him.

"Who rides the heavens to help you,
And in His excellency on the clouds.
The eternal God is your refuge,
And underneath are the everlasting arms..."
Deuteronomy 33:26-27

"Fear not, for I am with you;
Be not dismayed, for I am your God.
I will strengthen you, Yes I will help you.
I will uphold you with My righteous right hand."
Isaiah 41:10

"I Will Call Upon the Lord"

I will love you Lord, for all my days,
You are my strength and solid rock,
Lifting your Holy Name in praise,
You're my fortress strong, with Whom I walk.

I will call upon the Lord
Who is worthy to be praised,
Your Spirit on me is poured,
I worship your Holy ways.

My deliverer, in whose name I trust,
My protector and my mighty shield,
You are perfectly righteous, perfectly just,
My will to you, I forever yield.

I will call upon the Lord
Who is worthy to be praised,
Your Spirit on me is poured,
I worship your Holy ways.

You are the horn of my salvation,
My stronghold and my sanctuary,
Saving me from such deprivation,
My King, You are extraordinary.

I will call upon the Lord
Who is worthy to be praised,
Your Spirit on me is poured,
I worship your Holy ways.

Dear Lord,

You are our solid rock upon whom we depend. When we feel needy, you are always there, ready to help us with any trial or tribulation. We take comfort in your tender mercies. Thank you for being available to us day and night.

Amen

Day Fifteen

The Lord Almighty is His Name

Who is this mighty God that we worship? He is the "Great I AM", who alone is omnipotent (all-powerful), omniscient (all-knowing), omnipresent (forever with us), infinite, eternal, and forever my friend.

Our Lord is **"Omnipotent"**

"who being the brightness of His glory
and the express image of His person
and upholding all things by the word of His power..."
Hebrews1:1-3

"The heavens declare the glory of God
and the firmament declares His handiwork"
Psalm 19:1

"Alleluia! The Lord God Omnipotent reigns."
Revelation 19:6

"... His invisible attributes are clearly seen,
being understood by the things that are made,
even His eternal power and Godhead"
Romans 1:20

Our Lord is **"Omniscient"**

"For your Father knows all things
you have need of before you ask Him"
Matt 6:8

"The Lord knows the thoughts of man."
Psalm 94:11

"God is greater than our heart, and knows all things."
1 John 3:20

Our Lord is **"Omnipresent"**

"But will God indeed dwell on the earth?
Behold, heaven and the heaven of heavens
cannot contain You."
1 Kings 8:27

"Where shall I go from Your Spirit?
Or where can I flee from Your presence?
If I ascent into heaven, You are there;
If I make my bed in hell, behold, you are there.
If I take the wings of the morning,
and dwell in the uttermost parts of the sea,
even there Your hand shall lead me.
If I say 'Surely the darkness shall fall on me,'
even the night shall be light about me;
Indeed, the darkness shall not hide from You."
Psalm 139:7-12

Our Lord is "**Infinite**"

"Great is our Lord and mighty in power;
His understanding is infinite."
Psalm 147:5

<u>Our Lord is</u> **"Eternal"**

"Now to the King eternal, immortal,
invisible, to God who alone is wise,
be honor and glory forever and ever, Amen."
1 Timothy 1:17

so many more passages which describe the holy attributes and character of God. He is our all-in-all, the Alpha and Omega. To Him be power and glory forever.

"The Lord Almighty is His Name"

*"For I am the Lord, your God, who churns up the sea
so that its waves roar – the Lord Almighty is His name..."*
Isaiah 51:15

The Lord Almighty is His name,
Forever and always to be the same,
Author of life and infinite Lord,
Ruling the universe by His Word.

His power is manifest in His righteous right hand,
Seas will part at His command,
Yet agape love embraces His throne,
Making His Holy presence known.

He churns the seas making the waves to roar,
His majesty emanates forevermore,
Showing forth His mighty control,
Surrounding the depths of my very soul.

I praise His mighty and wonderful name,
Holiness surrounds a consuming flame,
Too perfect to ever comprehend,
My Abba, my Comforter, my dearest friend.

The Lord Almighty is His name,
The heavens cry out His great acclaim,
The Anointed One, the Sovereign Lamb,
The King of Kings, the Great I AM.

Dear Jesus,

You are truly the King of Kings
and Lord of Lords.
We worship Your holy name.
Although, You are all powerful,
completely holy and full of wisdom,
You take extreme delight in
honoring us with Your presence.
Amen

"O Lord, we have waited for You;
The desire of our soul is for Your name
And the remembrance of You.
With my soul I have desired
You in the night,
Yes, by my spirit within me
I will seek You early."
Isaiah 26: 8-9

Day Sixteen

The Fountain of the Water of Life

"As the deer pants for the streams of water,
So my soul pants for you, O God.
My soul thirsts for God, the Living God..."
Psalm 42:1 & 2

Although our God dwells in heavenly places, we still have immediate access to him at all times. He is never far from us, just a call away. He longs for our fellowship and desires for us to draw near to Him, as a father would for his beloved sons and daughters. He invites us to transcend the triviality of this finite world and see the true beauty of His divine dwelling place. We are always welcome there. He cherishes the time we spend with Him because He cares for us so much. Our prayers are forever a delight to His ear.

"I waited patiently for the Lord; and he inclined to me.
And heard my cry and brought me out of a horrible pit,
out of the miry clay, and set my feet upon a rock,
and established my steps.
He put a new song in my mouth"
Psalm 40:1-3

In 2 Chronicles 30:27, the faithful people of God cried out to the Lord... *"and their voice was heard and their prayer came up to His holy dwelling place, heaven."*

King David is described in the word of God as a man after God's own heart because he sought to both please God and to enter into His holy presence. Yes, we too, can dwell in the presence of God. According to the scriptures, we have direct access to the Father through His Son, Jesus Christ.

"For through Him (Jesus)
we have access by one Spirit
to the Father."
Ephesians 2:18

"The Fountain of the Water of Life"

"I am the Alpha and the Omega,
the beginning and the end,
I will give of the fountain of the water of life
freely to him who thirsts."
Revelation 21:6

In the midst of a desert, oh so dry,
Thirst wracked my withered soul,
My heart was faint and captured by,
A heat beyond control.

Then the One who is and was and will be,
Appeared in this barren place,
Offering living water to me
As I gazed upon His face.

The water came from a flowing fountain,
Magnificent to my sight,
Cascading from God's holy mountain,
A spring of great delight.

He who bore it was as a Lamb,
Full of glory and power,
The King of Kings, the Great I Am,
My fortress and Strong Tower.

"O Lord, please tell me what to do,
To partake of this river of life,
To fill my cup and my strength renew,
To no longer feel this strife.

With joy, The Glorious Lord replied,
"It is free to all to take,
the perfect gift, I will provide,
and never will forsake."

He handed me the flowing chalice,
I drank and became alive,
As I entered into the Sovereign's palace,
My spirit was revived.

From death to life, I breathed anew,
In the presence of the Living God,
My Savior, Lord and friend so true,
Whose love is shed abroad.

*"...because the love of God
is shed abroad in our hearts
through the Holy Ghost."
Romans 5:5*
KJV

Dear Lord,

Your living water continually refreshes
us with its cleansing and renewing flow.
It is given to us freely, just as
You gave it to
the woman at the well.
Thank you, Jesus.

Revelation 7:14 – 17 says,
"And He who sits on the throne
shall dwell among them.
They shall neither hunger anymore
nor thirst anymore;
The sun shall not strike them,
nor any heat;
For the lamb who is in the midst

of the throne will shepherd them
and lead them to
Fountains of Living Water."

Day Seventeen

The Yearning

"Because you have made the Lord,
who is my refuge,
Even the Most High, your dwelling place,
no evil shall befall you."
Psalm 91:9

Although our God dwells in heavenly places, we still have immediate access to him at all times. He is never far from us, just a call away. He desires our companionship and longs for us to draw near to Him, as a father would for his beloved sons and daughters. He invites us to transcend the triviality of this finite world and see the true beauty of His divine dwelling place. We are always welcome there. He cherishes the time we spend with Him because He loves us so much. Our prayers are forever a delight to His ear. Let our hearts be His dwelling place as He touches us with His unchanging love.

"I waited patiently for the Lord;
and he inclined to me.
And heard my cry and brought me out of a horrible pit,
out of the miry clay, and set my feet upon a rock,
and established my steps.
He put a new song in my mouth"
Psalm 40:1-3

In 2 Chronicles 30:27, the faithful people of God cried out to the Lord...

"and their voice was heard
and their prayer came up
to His holy dwelling place, heaven."

King David was described as a man after God's own heart because he sought to both please God and to enter into His holy presence. We too, can in fact dwell in the presence of God. According to the scriptures, we have direct access to the Father through His Son, Jesus Christ.

"For through Him (Jesus)
we have access by one Spirit to the Father."
Ephesians 2:18

"The Yearning"

"How lovely is Your dwelling place, O Lord Almighty!
My soul yearns, even faints for the courts of the Lord:
My heart and my flesh cry out
For the Living God..."
Psalm 84:1 & 2

O Living God, Lord of my soul,
The One Most High, my Rock so strong,
O Mighty One in full control,
To You I sing this song.

Every hour, I need Your power,
From the depths of my spirit I call your name,
Almighty God, my own strong tower,
Forever your praises I will proclaim.

My soul will ever yearn and faint,
For Your courts so grand and regal,
My heart and flesh feel no restraint,
As I soar on the wings of an eagle.

Your living water quenches my thirst,
As I ever seek Your face,
My Glorious God, I put you first,
You are my dwelling place.

"And He showed me a pure river of water of life,
clear as crystal, proceeding from
the throne of God
and of the Lamb."
Revelation 22:1

You are our dwelling place, O Lord!

We seek You with our whole heart
and long to be
in the shadow of Your wings.
Draw us near to you
as we pour out our hearts.
We lift this petition to Your
holy throne in anticipation
of Your response. You
are here for us always.

Day Eighteen

A Prayer to the God of My Life

My prayers continually ascend to my All in
All. Everything is from You, O God!

Our relationship with God is a two way street. Not only are we able to pray to Him, expressing our inner most thoughts but if we carefully listen, we can also hear his response to us. To some, prayer has become merely a wish list in which we petition for the material things we may want or need. But true prayer should be an act of worship and devotion to the Living God above, the One who cares for us like no other, the One who satisfies our longing soul and gives us peace.

"For He satisfies the longing soul,
and fills the hungry soul with goodness."
Psalm 107:9

Because of who God is and how He made us, we have a profound need for Him in our lives. We desire his presence and long to know Him intimately. Without this type of personal relationship, there is an enormous vacuum in our soul that nothing else can fill.

"As the deer pants for the water brooks,
So pants my soul for You, O God.
My soul thirsts for God,
for the living God."
Psalm 42:1-2

We can be certain that He is always there for us, beckoning us to draw near to Him, loving us with a love so deep that we are unable to fathom it. He truly desires our fellowship. Draw near to Him today.

"Yes I have loved you with an everlasting love;
Therefore with lovingkindness I have drawn you."
Jeremiah 31:3

"A Prayer to the God of My Life"

"Deep calls to deep in the roar of your waterfalls,
all Your waves and breakers have swept over me.
By day the Lord directs His love
At night His song is with me
A prayer to the God of my life..."
Psalm 42:7-8

In the roar of the waters, I hear your voice,
Speaking words of comfort to me,
From the depths of my heart I will rejoice,
Your love has set me free.

Sweeping over me are your mighty waves,
Washing me with living water,
Cleansing me with your blood that saves,
Calling me your beloved daughter.

By day I feel your love within,
Guiding me through every hour,
At night your love song will begin,
As I feel your strength and power.

I give you praise forevermore,
You save me from grief and strife,
From within my soul my prayer will pour,
"A prayer to the God of my life."

Oh God, mere words cannot express,
The thoughts within my heart,
Your love forever I will profess,
I just don't know where to start.

"I spread out my hands to You;
for my soul longs for You
like a thirsty land"
Psalm 143:6

Dear Lord,

We ask for a divine appointment
with You today.
You are the Father who loves us more than
words can ever begin to express.
Give us an impartation of your Holy presence.
Only You can fill the void in our lives.
You shower us with joy in our inner man
and reach deeply into our souls.
Thank you for the serene and
tranquil moments we spend with You.

Day Nineteen

The Wind

We are drawn to Your Spirit, as a moth is to the Light. The Holy Spirit is like the wind in a massive hurricane, surging powerfully, consuming us as we yield to Him, penetrating the inner depths of our being. He commands our attention like a heralding trumpet and buffets us in the direction of His choice. We cling to Him in times of trouble as He sweeps us away to His domain.

And at other times, He appears as a gentle cooling breeze, quietly refreshing our souls and tenderly whispering words of love in our ears. As He summons us into His presence, He calls us from the mediocrity of life's daily routine into the heavenly realm of His placid dwelling place. The Spirit is always available to us, ever wooing us to Him, yet we continually flee, in pursuit of the frivolities of earth.

"And the Spirit and the bride say 'Come!'
And let him who hears say, 'Come!'
And let him who thirsts come.
Whoever desires, let him take
of the water of life freely."
Revelation 22:17

The Spirit binds us to Himself and beckons His children to partake of His peace and revel in His Light. He is our constant Comforter and Helper.

"But the helper, the Holy Spirit
whom the Father will send in My name
will teach you all things and bring to your remembrance
all things that I said to you."
John 14:26

"I drew them with gentle cords,
with bands of love,
And I was to them as those
who take the yoke from their neck."
Hosea 11:4

"The Wind"

"Suddenly a sound,
like the blowing of a violent wind
came from heaven and filled the whole house
where they were sitting..."
Acts 2:2

His cooling touch upon my skin,
Blowing fiercely through my hair,
I feel His mighty power within,
Of His delightful presence I become aware.

It's the presence of the Spirit of God,
Much more than just a squall,
Blowing so powerfully as I trod,
I hear His awesome call.

Wind of life, Wind of fire,
A tempest full of wonder,
Clothe my soul in bright attire,
Let me hear Your thunder.

Tongues of fire upon my head,
The heavens open wide,
The glory of God has visited,
On me He will abide.

Without beginning and without end,
Both like a storm and gentle breeze,
His power I cannot comprehend,
As He churns the raging seas.

The outpouring of overwhelming love,
Transforming for all eternity,
Transcending everything above,
Encompassing infinity.

Holy Spirit, breathe on me,
Pour out Your full control,
Take over, set my spirit free,
Fill my hungry soul.

"The wind blows wherever it pleases.
You hear its sound
but cannot tell
where it comes from
or where it goes.
So it is with everyone
born of the Spirit..."
John 3:8

O Holy Spirit,

We ask for a fresh revelation of who You are.
You are our comforter, our helper
and our constant companion.
You are the gift of the Father,
speaking exclusively of the Son,
and filling our hearts with
love, joy and peace.
You always abide in us, teaching
us Your ways.
We love You.

Day Twenty

Your Word has Given Me Life

The word of God is alive and sharper than any two edged sword. It pierces the innermost recesses of our hearts, convicting us of our desperate need for God. The bible is God's instruction manual to introduce us to Himself and show us how we should live our lives on the earth. We think of life here as the ultimate reality, the only true and valid state of existence. But on the contrary, this life is only a temporary place, a stepping stone to the ultimate reality of eternity. This is why there are so many questions which seem to be unanswerable. But as we diligently search the word of God, we find those answers and along with them, a peace and joy which cannot be explained in human terms.

"Your words were found and I ate them
and Your word was to me
the joy and rejoicing of my heart."
Jeremiah 15:16

Our history reveals decades in which the human race has chosen to separate itself from God. In doing this, we have distanced ourselves from Him and in turn have placed him in the same category with myth or fantasy. We are so quick to dismiss His word as invalid, when it is set before us by God Himself, as a beacon, leading the way to truth. If only we would take the time as did Martin Luther to delve into this great work and see for ourselves the ultimate truth which lies within its pages; the eternal truth and only hope for mankind.

"For whatever things were written before
were written for our learning that we through patience
and comfort of the scriptures might have hope"
Romans 15:4

"I will delight myself in Your statutes;
I will not forget Your word."
Psalm 119:16

"I will never forget your precepts,
for by them You have given me life."
Psalm 119:93

Your Word has Given Me Life

"Remember the word to Your servant,
Upon which You have caused me to hope,
This is my comfort in my affliction,
For Your word has given me life."
Psalm 119:49-50

It is in Your word that I receive great hope,
Your word is a lamp unto my feet,
Through times of trouble I now can cope,
Never turning my back on sin's defeat.

Your Word is my comfort in all affliction,
Each precept I hold in the depths of my soul,
Giving power, strength and great conviction,
Speaking the truth that makes me whole.

You are the Truth, the Life, the Way
Forever I will seek your face,
Trusting completely every day,
To receive Your unconditional grace.

You are my joy, my peace, my song,
Taking away the grief and strife,
To You forever I will belong,
Because Your word has given me life.

A powerful light that illumines the dark,
Directing my path from all in the way,
Guiding my feet, as I embark,
Into a realm as bright as day.

"Your word is a lamp unto my feet.
And a light to my path."
Psalm 119:105

Dear Lord,

You have told us in Psalm 138:2 that You
have magnified Your word above Your name.
The first chapter of John tells
us that you are the Word.
"In the beginning was the Word
and the Word was with God
and the Word Was God...
He was in the beginning with God. All things
were made by Him, and without Him nothing
was made that was made. In Him was life
and the life was the light of men... and the
Word became flesh and dwelt among us, and
we beheld His glory, the glory as of the only
begotten of the Father, full of grace and truth."

Day Twenty One

My Thanksgiving Prayer

When we ponder on of all the wonderful things God has given us, our hearts well up with thanksgiving. We are blessed with life, love, family and most of all fellowship with a loving God. It is human nature to take these blessings for granted as we go through our daily schedule, consumed with superficial activities. But if we look at life in view of eternity, we realize just how meaningless some things are in the long run. Of course a variety of these things are essential to our survival but in comparison, the reality of God's presence is far more significant.

"For with You is the fountain of life,
In Your light we see light."
Psalm 36:9

"Therefore I will give thanks to You, O Lord...
And give You praise."
Psalm 18:49

Have you ever loved someone and in your desire to express that love, given them an expensive gift? But instead of being appreciative, they tossed it aside, as if it had no value to them. This is what God goes through with us, His ungrateful children. He has given us the gift of His Son and the assurance of heaven for all eternity yet we prefer to cast it all aside in search of the vain trifles of life on earth. Take some time now to ponder the many gifts God has bestowed to us.

"Oh, give thanks to the Lord!
Call upon His name;
Make known His deeds among the peoples!
Sing to Him, sing psalms to Him;
Talk of his wondrous works!
Glory in His holy name."
Psalm 105:1-3

"My Thanksgiving Prayer"

"Enter into His gates with thanksgiving,
and into His courts with praise,
Be thankful to Him and bless His name..."
Psalm 100:4

My thanks pour forth from deep within,
From the depths of my soul my prayers will soar,
I hardly know where to begin,
From the bottom of my heart I thank You for...

Your eternal love, Your immeasurable grace,
Which helps me through the darkest of nights,
Your sheltering mercy, Your loving embrace,
Guiding us onward to infinite heights.

Your righteous right hand, Your radiant face,
The sound of Your voice as rushing waters,
A brilliance that time cannot erase,
Love's shining light to Your sons and daughters.

You cradle us tenderly in outstretched arms,
A Father whose love we can't comprehend,
Protecting us peacefully from all harm,
Throughout eternity, world without end.

You gave salvation freely to man,
A greater love could not be won,
You gave us redemption, it was Your plan,
Because You gave Your only Son.

"Thanks be to God for His incredible gift."
2 Corinthians 9:15

Dear Lord,

Your gifts to us are beyond measure.
But the greatest gift of all is Your Son.
"God has given us eternal life, and this
life is in His Son. He who has the
Son has life; he who does not have the
Son of God does not have life."

1 John 5:11

Day Twenty Two

From Waves of Anguish to Glorious Light

Have you ever been trapped within a sea of negativity and depression, unable to escape through the power of your own strength? This scenario happens to some of us more often than others but we need to know that God is continually with us in this and His marvelous Light is readily available to us the minute we call on His name. His word declares:

"Hear me when I call, O God of my righteousness!
You have relieved me in my distress;
Have mercy on me and hear my prayer."
Psalm 4:1

"Thus my heart was grieved and I was vexed in my mind...
Nevertheless I am continually with You;
You hold me by my right hand.
You will guide me with Your counsel, and
afterward receive me to glory..."
Psalm 73:21, 23, 24

"My flesh and my heart fail; But God is the strength
Of my heart and portion forever."
Psalm 73:26

Sometimes we get bogged down with the cares of this world and consequently, we are blinded to God's light streaming down from heaven. We tend to feel isolated from Him and powerless to grasp His awaiting hand. It is as if He is just beyond the reach of our outstretched arms, fading, gradually into the distance. But He tells us He will never leave us and His word is faithful and true. It is impossible for God to lie.

*"For He Himself has said, 'I will never
Leave you or forsake you.'"*
Hebrews 13:5

*"And lo, I am with you always,
Even to the end of the age."*
Matthew 28:20

"From Waves of Anguish to Glorious Light"

A sea of obscurity surrounded my soul,
Great tempests caused the waves to crash,
Monstrous winds whipped beyond control,
As the last of my hopes began to dash.

Shadowy figures clutched at my core,
Outstretched hands seized my captive heart,
Dragging me downward to the ocean floor,
Tearing my sinking world apart.

I prayed, I sobbed and shrieked Your name,
From afar a beacon led the way,
God's wondrous brilliance, His eternal flame,
Guided me forward to the light of day.

Invisible footprints directed my path,
Your light gleamed brightly as I tried to grope,
Your loving hand was there to grasp,
Your luminous presence gave me hope.

"Your path led through the sea,
Your ways through the mighty waters,
Though Your footprints were not seen..."
Psalm 77:19

Yes, You are always there, O Lord,

leading and guiding us by the
power of Your Spirit,
showing us the path back to You.
Our eyes are forever on You, God.
You let us know you are
always there for us and
that not one hair can fall from our head
without Your knowledge.
"Surely goodness and mercy shall
Follow me all the days of my life;
And I will dwell in the house
of the Lord forever"

Psalm 23:6

Day Twenty Three

While Shining Like Stars...

In Daniel chapter 12, we read that in the time of the end, the wise and the righteous will shine like stars. We will be surrounded in God's glory for all eternity, partaking of the true love and joy which comes from being in His amazing presence.

> *"Those who are wise shall shine*
> *like the brightness of the firmament,*
> *and those who turn many to righteousness*
> *like the stars forever and ever."*
> *Daniel 12:3*

What a glorious day that will be! We will radiate with the light of the Lord and glow like the rays of the sun. We will be like the Seraphim whose name in the original language is "burning ones," ablaze with fire but not being consumed.

> *"Arise, shine; for your light has come!*
> *And the glory of the Lord is risen upon you,*
> *For behold, the darkness shall cover the earth,*
> *And deep darkness the people;*
> *But the Lord will arise over you,*
> *And His glory will be seen upon you."*
> *Isaiah 60: 1-2*

It is inconceivable that one day we will have glorified bodies that will resemble the majestic body of Jesus. We will shine like the sun and take on a radiance that will be mind boggling.

> *"For our citizenship is in heaven,*
> *from which we also eagerly wait for the Savior,*
> *the Lord Jesus Christ,*
> *Who will transform our lowly body that it may*

Be conformed to His glorious body..."
Philippians 3:21

"Beloved, now we are children of God;
And it has not yet been revealed what we shall be,
But we know that when he is revealed,
We shall be like Him, for we shall see Him as He is."
1 John 3:2

While Shining Like Stars

"At that time, Michael shall stand up,
the great prince who stands watch
over the sons of your people;
and there shall be a time of trouble,
such as never was since there was a nation,
even to that time. And at that time
your people shall be delivered,
everyone who is found written in the book.
And many of those who sleep
in the dust of the earth shall awake.
Some to everlasting life,
some to shame and everlasting contempt.
Those who are wise shall shine
like the brightness of the firmament,
and those who turn many to righteousness
like the stars forever and ever."
Daniel 12:1-3

The Archangel Michael at the time of the end,
Shall stand up and declare who he protects and defends,
There will be trouble, calamity and great tribulation,
Such as never existed since there was a nation.

But do not fear,
For your God draws near,
His righteous right hand,
Fulfills all that He planned.

At that time your people shall be delivered,
While enemies and foes will quake and quiver,
And all whose names are written in the book,
Will forever abide with their God, Come, look!

Many who sleep in the dust shall awake,
Some of everlasting life will partake,
But others to shame,
and the sound of their name,
Will echo contempt,
They will not be exempt.
A consuming fire to some,
His great wrath will come,

But others will know His everlasting love,
To be held by the Lion, the Lamb and the Dove,
The wise will shine with the brightness of the Lord,
Carrying His helmet, bearing His sword.

The wise will shine with His radiant light,
Beholding His Glory so exceedingly bright,
Turning many to righteousness, will be their endeavor,
While shining like stars, forever and ever.

Awesome God,

You are the revealer of all things.
Your light shines ever before us,
displaying to Your children, Your agape love.
Your delight is in Your people
as You carry us the wings of the wind.

"Bless the Lord, O my soul!
O Lord, my God, You are very great:
You are clothed with honor and majesty,
Who cover yourself with light
As with a garment,
Who stretch out the heavens like a curtain...
Who makes the clouds His chariot,
Who walks on the wings of the wind..."
Psalm 104:1 - 3

Day Twenty Four

Lights in the World

The word of God tells us in many passages that we need to let the light of Jesus shine brightly through us, reflecting His glory to others. We are ambassadors who are given the responsibility to share the good news of the gospel and to let our conduct not have an adverse effect on our testimony. When the world looks at us, we want them to see Jesus and not just a mirror image of themselves. God has called us forth to be separate from the world.

"Do not love the world or the things in the world.
If anyone love the world,
The love of the Father is not in Him
1 John 2:15

"Come out from among them
and be separate says the Lord
2 Corinthians 6:17

"I beseech you therefore, brethren by the mercies of God,
that you present your bodies a living sacrifice,
holy, acceptable to God, which is your reasonable service.
And do not be conformed to this world but be transformed
by the renewing of your minds that you
may prove what is that good
and acceptable and perfect will of God."
Romans 12: 1-2

God has called us to be separate from the world, consecrated to Him and holy.

"And you shall be holy to Me, for I the Lord am holy,
and have separated you from the peoples,
that you should be mine."
Leviticus 20:26

"But as he who called you is holy,
You also be holy in all your conduct
Because it is written, 'Be holy for I am holy."
1 Peter 1:15

"Lights in the World"

*"...among whom you shine as lights in the world,
holding fast the word of life..."*
Philippians 2:15

In the midst of a crooked and perverse generation,
You shine as the beams of glory,
Proclaiming God's love and restoration,
Revealing His awesome story.

Holding fast to the word of life,
A brilliant beacon to the lost,
A sword that pierces like the sharpest knife,
The flame of Pentecost.

Let us shine so boldly for all to see,
Like a blaze within the night,
The shining lamp of victory,
Whose oil is burning bright.

Anointed oil, consuming fire,
Let it burn forevermore,
Our robes will glow in white attire,
As we ascend to heaven's shore.

Let heaven and earth view only <u>Your</u> light,
For without you we are naught,
Let Your spirit unveil this blinding sight,
Revealing Your fire, so hot.

"For our God is a consuming fire..."
Hebrews 12:29

Dear Lord,

You are a consuming fire, yet
so much Light radiates down to us
from Your dwelling place.
You have loved us with an everlasting love
and have given us the eternal flame
of Your Spirit to dwell deeply
within our being.

"I will love You, O Lord, my strength.
The Lord is my rock and my
fortress and my deliverer;
My God, my strength in whom I will trust;
My shield and the horn of my
salvation, my stronghold.
I will call on the Lord who
is worthy to be raised."
Psalm 18:1 - 3

Day Twenty Five

My Place of Shelter

Imagine being at sea in a disabled boat, being towed to safety by the Coast Guard. Suddenly a violent storm arises, the rope breaks and your boat is floundering alone in the midst of the treacherous waves. The darkness envelopes you and you are caught up tightly in the grip of fear. The Bible puts it this way:

"For my heart is in anguish within me,
the terrors of death assail me,
Fear and trembling have beset me,
horror has overwhelmed me.
I said 'Oh that I had the wings of a dove!
And would fly away
And be at rest- I would flee far away
and stay in the desert;
I would hurry to my place of shelter,
far from the tempest and storm."
Psalm 55:4-8

When we encounter a situation like this, we can be assured at all times that our Lord is with us and will protect us. His mighty hand and outstretched arm shields us from all harm as we are hidden within the shadows of His wings. He is our good shepherd who gives us peace.

"The Lord is my Shepherd; I shall not want.
He makes me to lie down in green pastures;
He leads me beside the still waters. He restores my soul.
He leads me in the path of righteousness for His name's sake.
Yea, though I walk through the valley of the shadow
of death, I will fear no evil; For You are with me;
Your rod and your staff, they comfort me.
You prepare a table before me in the presence of my enemies;

You anoint my head with oil; my cup runs over.
Surely goodness and mercy shall follow me all the days of my life;
And I will dwell in the House of the Lord forever."
Psalm 23

When David was surrounded by his enemies, he knew God was there to sustain him. We too can have this confidence, knowing that He is always with us.

"But You, O Lord are a shield for me,
My glory and the One who lifts up my head.
I cried to the Lord with my voice
And He heard me from His holy hill."
Psalm 3:3-4

"My Place of Shelter"

"For You have been a shelter for me,
A strong tower from the enemy.
I will abide in Your tabernacle forever;
I will trust in the shelter of Your wings."
Psalm 61:3-4

You, O Lord, are my place of shelter,
You are my strength and shield,
You are the Rock where I cast my anchor,
To You I forever yield.

With storms round about,
Howling winds ever shout,
You are the One who saves me from death,
When the tempest will rage,
At the end of the age,
You are near as we take our last breath.

Your comfort surrounds us,
Your power astounds us,
Your love is complete in Your haven of rest,
All terror has fled, by the blood that You shed,
In Your arms we are joyfully blessed.

Nevermore to feel fear,
Only wonders appear,
As I cast all my crowns at Your feet with delight,
To forever sing praise,
For now and always,
In Your presence of Glorious Light.

Lord,

Your presence is ever near to us.
Forever you connect us to Your heart and
Bind us to Yourself in love.

"You shall love the Lord your God with all
your heart, with all your soul, and with all
your strength. And these words I command you
today shall be in your heart. You shall teach
them diligently to your children, and shall talk
of them when you sit in your house, when you
walk by the way, when you lie down, and when
you rise up. You shall bind them as a sign
on your hand, and they shall be as frontlets
between your eyes. You shall write them on the
doorposts of your house, and on your gates."
Deuteronomy 6: 4 - 9

Day Twenty Six

Seek My Face

"Seek the Lord and His strength;
Seek His face forevermore."
Psalm 105:4

What happens when we truly seek the face of the Lord? He has promised us in His word that He will manifest His presence to us in a powerful way. He is the all-encompassing creator of the universe yet can be as close to us as our very own breath. He sees all, knows all and is our all in all. He will take us as deeply into His soul as we will allow Him. He beckons us to draw near but fear of the unknown sometimes makes us shy away. But please know that we can trust Him with our hearts because He is the lover of our soul.

I remember when I was first introduced to Him. He was a loving and powerful acquaintance. I was in deep awe of Him as I prayed to Him and beheld His glorious creation. Then the more time I spent with Him, the better I began to know Him, really know Him and His unconditional love for me. He was always there to comfort and console me. He understood the inner workings of my soul and was my constant companion. How easy it is to love him when He changes from acquaintance to friend.

"Come unto Me, all you who are weary and heavy laden.
And I will give you rest. Take my yoke
upon you and learn from Me,
For I am gentle and lowly in heart, and
you will find rest for your souls.
For My yoke is easy and My burden is light.
Matthew 11: 28-30

"Lord, You have been our dwelling place in all generations.
Before the mountains were brought forth,
Or ever You had formed the earth and the world,
From everlasting to everlasting,
You are God."
Psalm 90: 1-2

"Seek My Face"

"When You said 'Seek My face,'
my heart said to You,
"Your face, Lord, I will seek"
Psalm 27:8

By Your love, You have drawn me near to You,
Your closeness fills my heart,
As I ever turn my ear to You,
Great tenderness, You impart.

Because You have drawn me, I seek Your face,
The most glorious face of all,
I am captured by your endless grace,
I hear Your gentle call.

A call that warms me in the night,
When all is dark, I see Your light,
I will seek Your face forevermore,
As I wander through Your open door.

To behold Your glory, to view Your splendor,
Is to walk within Your light,
To You my all, I will surrender,
I am astounded by Your might.

"For He satisfies the longing soul,
And fills the hungry soul with goodness."
Psalm 107:9

Dear Lord,

Thank you for revealing your heart to those
who diligently seek after you.
This journey with You
has been filled with life,
adventure and exceeding love.
In the beginning, before I
knew You completely,
I was in awe of You
but also experienced great fear
at the very thought of You.
But 1 John 4:18 tells me that,
"There is no fear in love;
but perfect love casts out fear."

Day Twenty Seven

The Righteous Will Shine

"But you are a chosen generation, a royal priesthood,
A holy nation, His own special people,
That you may proclaim the praises of Him
Who called you out of darkness
Into His marvelous light."
1 Peter 2:9

We are called of God to enter into His holy presence by the precious blood of His Son, Jesus Christ, who died in our place that we may inherit eternal life. John 3: 15 and 16 says: *"For God so loved the world that He gave His only begotten Son, that whoever believes in Him should not perish but have everlasting life."*

Matthew 1: 13:43 says: *"The righteous will shine forth as the sun in the kingdom of their father."* We as believers in Jesus are righteous in God's sight not through anything we have done on our own but because through Jesus' death we are declared to have the righteousness of God imputed to us.

"For He (God) made Him who knew no sin (Jesus),
To be sin for us that we might become
the righteousness
Of God in Him"
2 Corinthians 5:21

"But now the righteousness of God apart
from the law is revealed,
Being witnessed by the Law and the Prophets,
Even the righteousness of God through faith in Jesus Christ,
To all and on all who believe. For there is no difference;

181

For all have sinned and fall short of the glory of God,
Being justified freely by His grace
Through the redemption that is in Christ Jesus."
Romans 3:21-24

"The Righteous Will Shine"

*"The righteous will shine forth as the sun
in the kingdom of their Father."*
Matthew 13:43

In the field of the world, the seeds are sown,
The seeds of the wheat and the tares,
The entire countryside is overgrown,
As the reaper's trumpet blares.

The wicked ones are set ablaze,
Within the furnace of fire,
While the wheat prepares for better days,
And receive their heart's desire.

The righteous will shine forth as the brilliant sun,
In the kingdom of their God,
Their glorious joy has just begun,
For eternity they will applaud.

Their shimmering light will never fade,
Surrounded by tender devotion,
Luminous beams forever displayed,
Glimmering stars in motion.

From night to day, in full array,
They bow at Jesus' throne,
The Truth, the Life, the perfect Way,
The magnificent Cornerstone.

Dear Jesus,

You are the only righteous One.
You shine forth, full of glory,
for all creation to behold.
This is why you have called us
to your righteousness.
"Do all things without
complaining and disputing,
that you may become blameless and harmless
children of God
without fault in the midst of a crooked
and perverse generation,
among whom you shine as lights in the world,
holding fast the word of life."
Philippians 2: 14 - 16

Day Twenty Eight

Your Bearer of Light

Sometimes, no matter how hard we try to seek God's presence and Light, it evades us. We may long for God's fellowship yet it seems to be just out of reach. At times like these, we must call on the Holy Spirit for help. When Jesus rose again, He sent a Comforter and Helper, the Holy Spirit, to minister to us when we lose our way and things get rough.

"And I pray the Father, and He will give you
Another Helper, that He may abide with you forever –
The Spirit of truth, whom the world cannot receive,
Because it neither sees Him nor knows Him;
But you know Him, for He dwells with you
And will be in you. I will not leave you orphans;
I will come to you."
John 14:16-18

"These things I have spoken to you
while being present with you.
But the Helper, the Holy Spirit,
whom the Father will send in My name,
He will teach you all things
and bring to your remembrance
All things that I said to you.
Peace I leave with you;
Not as the world gives do I give to you.
Let not your heart be troubled
Neither let it be afraid."
John 14:25-27

Once we know Jesus as our personal savior, the Holy Spirit lives inside us as a helper and guide. John 16:13 tells us: *"However when He, the Spirit of truth, has come, He will guide you into all truth."*

Yes, the third person of the trinity dwells with us showing us God's love and enables us to walk worthy of the calling of God.

> *"that you may walk worthy of the Lord, fully pleasing Him,*
> *Being fruitful in every good work and increasing*
> *In the knowledge of God; strengthened with all might,*
> *According to His glorious power..."*
> *Colossians 1:10-11*

The Holy Spirit not only indwells us but He also empowers us and enables us to do the things of God. There are two very important passages that prove to us that in our own fleshly power we can do nothing. When we are born again we are provided with a new nature but since we still have our fleshly body we still have our natural man who is corrupt because of the fall of Adam.

> *"Without You we can do nothing."*
> *John 15:5*

> *"I can do <u>all things</u>*
> *through Christ who strengthens me."*
> *Philippians 4:13*

Your Bearer of Light

Sitting alone on a cloudy day,
Wishing again for skies of blue,
In the depths of my heart my soul would pray,
That I could hear a word from You.

Then You sent a bearer of Your light,
To shine illuminating rays,
To open my eyes, to give me sight,
To penetrate the misty haze.

Through You was brought Your confirmation,
Encouragement was the gift You chose,
To manifest Your proclamation,
Opening a door that once was closed.

Your name I will forever glorify,
On my lips will be Your constant praise,
Your majestic splendor I magnify,
Once again You've set my heart ablaze.

"O send me Your light and Your truth!
Let them lead me; let them bring me to Your holy hill
and to Your tabernacle.
Then I will go to the mountain of God,
To God my exceeding joy;
And on the harp I will praise You, O God, my God."
Psalm 43:3

Heavenly Father,

We request that You grant to us
What is listed in the following scripture:

"The Lord bless you and keep you;
The Lord make His face
Shine upon you,
The Lord lift up His countenance
upon you,
And give you peace."

Numbers 6: 24 - 26

Day Twenty Nine

His Eyes Like a Flame of Fire...

There are numerous descriptions of our Savior, Jesus Christ listed throughout the bible. Everything from a gentle lamb, a fierce lion, a lowly carpenter to the reigning king, but one of my favorites is described in the book of Revelation. When the apostle John was given the privilege of seeing our Lord in the Spirit, he wrote these words in Revelation 1:9 – 16:

> *"I, John, both your brother and companion in the*
> *tribulation and the kingdom and patience*
> *of Jesus Christ, was on the island which is called Patmos*
> *for the word of God and the testimony*
> *of Jesus Christ. I was in the Spirit*
> *on the Lord's day, and I heard behind me*
> *a loud voice, as of a trumpet, saying,*
> *'I am the Alpha and the Omega,*
> *The first and the last and what you see write in a book...*
> *Then I turned to see the voice that spoke with me.*
> *And having turned I saw seven golden lampstand,*
> *and in the midst of the seven lampstands*
> *One like the Son of Man, clothed with a garment down to His feet*
> *and girded about the chest with a golden band.*
> *His head and hair were white like wool,*
> *as white as snow and His eyes like a flame of fire;*
> *His feet were like fine brass, as refined in a furnace,*
> *and His voice as the sound of many waters;*
> *He had in His right hand seven stars,*
> *out of His mouth went a sharp two-edged sword,*
> *and His countenance was like the sun shining in its strength."*

What a magnificent portrait of our Lord and Savior, Jesus Christ, who is truly the light of the world. We see Him here in all His glory manifesting His mighty character, much in the same way God, the

Father was depicted in Exodus 33, when He showed His partial glory to Moses on the mountain. There is a reason for this. Jesus is described in Colossians 1: 15-17 in the following way:

"He (Jesus) is the image of the invisible God,
The firstborn over all creation.
For by Him all things were created
That are in heaven and that are on earth,
Visible and invisible,
Whether thrones or dominions
Or principalities or powers.
All things were created through Him and for Him.
And He is before all things,
And in Him all things consist."

Jesus, the image of the invisible God

The invisible God cannot be seen,
His Spirit is outside the material,
Beyond the chromosome, preceding the gene,
Existing alongside the ethereal.

We dwell on earth within the perceivable,
Not understanding the presence of God,
His ways to us are inconceivable,
Defined by Aaron's rod.

And that is why our Savior came,
To bridge mortal man to the God immortal,
To take away our sin and blame,
Opening the way to heaven's portal.

His brilliant light reflects His devotion,
His love echoes through eternity,
His peace is like a tranquil ocean,
Farther than the eye can see.

"Now to the King eternal,
Immortal, invisible,
To God who alone is wise,
Be honor and glory, forever and ever,
Amen."

1 Timothy 1:17

Dear Lord,

Show us your brilliance and transform
us into your image, as we
diligently seek Your face.
Our desire is to be captured by your
shining light reflecting in our hearts.

"Your way was in the sea,
Your path in the great waters,
And Your footsteps were not known."
Psalm 77:19

Day Thirty

The Light of the World

"I am the light of the world.
He who follows Me shall not walk in darkness,
But have the light of life"
John 8:12

Long ago, before the fall of man, the world was filled with God's light. But through sin, darkness and death entered the world and the light faded, giving way to hopelessness and despair. This was not God's plan. Light had to be re-ignited. When He sent His Son to be born in a manger the first sign of this light was the star in the east, leading the wise men to the place of Jesus' birth. Another sign of light was mentioned in Luke chapter eight when an angel of the Lord stood before the shepherds "and the glory of the Lord shone around them". Thus our Savior made his journey from a humble birth to glory unspeakable as is described in the book of Revelation.

"One like the Son of man clothed with a garment
down to His feet and girded about the chest with a golden band.
His head and hair were like wool, as white as snow
and His eyes like a flame of fire; His feet were like brass,
as if refined in a furnace,
and His voice as the sound of many waters;
He had in His right hand seven stars,
out of His mouth went a two-edged sword,
and His countenance was like the sun shining in its strength."
Revelation 1:13-16

In the first chapter of Revelation, the apostle John beheld Jesus Christ in all His glory. The magnificent splendor of His presence was so intense that John fell on his face as a dead man. The presence of the glory of God could not be endured by the sight of men. That day will come when we are before Him, face to face.

"For now we see in a mirror, dimly,
but then face to face. Now I know in part
but then I shall know just as also I am known."
1 Corinthians 13:12

"In this the love of God was manifested toward us,
That God has sent His only begotten Son
Into the world that we might live through Him." 1 John 4:9

"The Light of the World"

"For You are my lamp, O Lord;
The Lord shall enlighten my darkness."
2 Samuel 22:29

On the earth there is no greater light,
Than the blazing sun above,
But God's Light of the world is more than bright,
It's full of His wondrous love.

The light of the world is Jesus our Lord,
Shining brilliantly out of the dark,
He casts out darkness through the power of His word,
Igniting the flames with His spark.

Because of Him I live my life anew,
Wrapped in His glorious Light,
His omnipotent presence I will always pursue,
It is forever within my sight.

He shows me the way, through the miry clay,
Into the realm of His radiant beams,
Forever I'll stay, enveloped by day,
While He protects, delivers, redeems.

"I am the light of the world.
He who follows Me shall not walk in darkness,
But have the light of life"
John 8:12

Wonderful Lord,

You are the Light that shines
Out of darkness, that illuminates
Your goodness, righteousness and love
To a sick and jaded world.

2 Corinthians 4:6 says:
"For it is the God who commanded
Light to shine out of darkness,
Who has shone in our hearts
to give the light
of the knowledge of the glory of God
In the face of Jesus Christ."

Day Thirty One

"God is Light"

"This is the message that we have heard
from Him and declare to you,
that God is light and in Him is no darkness at all.
If we say that we have fellowship with Him,
and walk in darkness, we lie and do not practice the truth.
but if we walk in the light as He is in the light, we have fellowship
with one another and the blood of Jesus Christ,
His Son cleanses us from all sin." I John 1:5-7

Although God dwells in "unapproachable light", that very Light visited us here on earth in the person of Jesus Christ, the second person of the trinity, who through His perfect sacrifice reconciled us to God. Although it was a horrific and painful sacrifice, Jesus did it willingly in order that we could be restored through His blood enabling us to stand in the presence of God for all eternity. He bridged the gap from outer darkness to everlasting light and did it all because of His great love for us.

"But God demonstrates His love toward us,
In that while we were still sinners, Christ died for us."
Romans 5:8

"I am the Light of the world. He who follows Me
Shall not walk in darkness but have the light of life."
John 8:12

"Who has blessed us with every spiritual
blessing in the heavenly places in Christ,
just as He chose us in Him before the foundation of the earth,
that we should be holy and without blame
before Him in love, having predestined us to adoption as sons
by Jesus Christ Himself, according to the good pleasure of His will,

205

to the praise of the glory of His grace
by which He made us accepted in the Beloved.
in Him we have redemption through His
blood, the forgiveness of sins,
according to the riches of His grace."
Ephesians 1:3-6

We are children of God through Jesus Christ and have been transformed from shadows to Shekinah through Him. There was nothing we could do of ourselves to merit this, but He did it all.

"That was the true light which
Gives light to every man
Coming into the world."
John 1:9

"God is Light"

You, O Lord, are the brightest of lights,
You radiate the sphere of the living,
Guiding us through the darkest of nights,
Flooding our hearts with thanksgiving.

None can compare to Your shining brilliance,
Radiance illuminates from your face,
Forever, You abide in grand resilience,
Imparting to us Your astounding grace.

Our fellowship with You will never cease,
As we walk in Your light forevermore,
Your love covers us with overwhelming peace,
On Your wings we ever soar.

We were chosen before the foundation of the earth,
To have God's righteousness through His Son,
Reconciled to the Father by our second birth,
Through Him our redemption is done.

"Most assuredly, I say to you,
Unless one is born again,
He cannot see the kingdom of God."
John 3:3

Heavenly Father,

We ask that Your light illuminate our hearts,
reflecting Your character in our lives.
Our desire is for others to see You instead us.
Thank you for your great love,
enabling the redemption and salvation
of our souls. . .
In the precious name of
Your Son, Jesus Christ.

Amen.

"And all these blessings
shall come upon you
and overtake you
because you obey the voice
of the Lord your God."

Deuteronomy 28:2

CPSIA information can be obtained at www.ICGtesting.com
Printed in the USA
LVOW12s2327200214

374557LV00004B/7/P